SHAKESPEARE FOR EVERYONE

THE
MERCHANT OF VENICE

By Jennifer Mulherin   *Illustrations by* Norman Bancroft-Hunt
CHERRYTREE BOOKS

Author's note

There is no substitute for seeing the plays of Shakespeare performed. Only then can you really understand why Shakespeare is our greatest dramatist and poet. This book simply gives you the background to the play and tells you about the story and characters. It will, I hope, encourage you to see the play.

A Cherrytree Book

Designed and produced by
A S Publishing

First published 1988
by Cherrytree Press Ltd
a subsidiary of
The Chivers Company Ltd
Windsor Bridge Road
Bath, Avon BA2 3AX

Copyright © Cherrytree Press Ltd 1988

British Library Cataloguing in Publication Data

Mulherin, Jennifer
    The merchant of Venice.
    1. Drama in English. Shakespeare, William.
    Merchant of Venice – Study outlines
    I. Title   II. Bancroft-Hunt, Norman
    822.3'3

    ISBN 0-7451-5019-5

Printed in Hong Kong by Colorcraft Ltd

Contents

Seafaring adventurers and The Merchant of Venice

Nowadays we tend to think of traders and merchants as ordinary unadventurous people, but in Shakespeare's day they were great heroes. They ventured on the high seas,

Sir Walter Raleigh with his son. Raleigh was a famous courtier in Elizabethan times, who, it is said, gallantly laid down his cloak on a muddy patch at Greenwich for the Queen to step on. Raleigh took part in a number of voyages of discovery, and invested an enormous amount of money in setting up the colony of Virginia.

voyaging to exotic and foreign lands in search of trade or treasure. They took risks which often paid off, and sometimes did not. However, without them England would not have been the great trading nation that it was in Elizabeth I's time.

Merchant adventurers

Merchants such as Antonio were not very different from explorers, and their exploits and adventures were of special interest to the Elizabethans. They travelled to lands such as Russia, Turkey and the Middle East. They also opened up new sea routes to the New World of North and South America, and explored the coastlines of Africa, India and the

This is a view of Goa in India in 1635. Goa was an important trading post for Portuguese seamen and merchants. In the early years of the 17th century, the English East India Company likewise established trade links with India on the mainland at Calcutta, and with the Spice Islands of the East Indies.

islands of the East Indies. Their purpose was to set up trade with these far-flung lands and to bring back exotic spices, foodstuffs or treasures, just as the Spaniards had done in the early part of the century.

How voyages were financed

Companies were set up to finance these ventures. Although only the fairly rich could afford to buy shares in these companies, many people invested their entire fortune. Sir Humphrey Gilbert, an Elizabethan courtier and the half-brother of Sir Walter Raleigh, lost not only his own inherited wealth but also his wife's money in a series of disastrous ventures.

One of the first companies to be set up was the Russian Company. This was founded in 1553 with £6000 raised by its 200 or so members. Out of the three ships that set sail for Russia, two were frozen up before they reached the White Sea. Fortunately, the third arrived safely at Archangel, the Russian port on the Arctic. England was the first country in those days to open up trade with Russia and the company made considerable profits for its shareholders.

The slave trade

English adventurers had already explored the coast of Guinea in Africa in Henry VIII's reign and brought back gold dust and ivory. Sir John Hawkins found another shameful source of wealth here – in human beings. He made a fortune transporting African slaves to work as labourers in the New World, and proudly displayed an African slave, bound with a cord, on his coat of arms.

The exploits of Sir Francis Drake

Sir Francis Drake is one of the greatest heroes in English history, who is remembered for defeating the Spanish

This miniature shows Sir Francis Drake, one of the great heroes of English history. Drake, who commanded the fleet which destroyed the Spanish Armada, has been described by one historian as just 'a merchant seaman commissioned by the Crown in a crisis.'

5

Armada. Before that, however, he had been something of a pirate. He sailed the Spanish Main in the West Indies, capturing ships laden with treasure on their way back to Spain. Although sea dogs like Drake risked torture and even death if they were caught, the profits were worth it. Being loyal Protestants, too, they thought they were doing God's work in taking ships and treasure from Catholic Spain.

A voyage round the world

Drake's voyage in 1577 to open up the Pacific was backed by a small company of merchant adventurers, who raised the modest sum of £6000. Despite the loss of men and ships in the perils of the voyage, Drake with one ship and 80 men held on boldly to reach the coast of Chile and Peru. Here they found unguarded Spanish treasures and Drake loaded his boat with gold, silver, pearls, emeralds and diamonds.

With spoils of more than half a million pounds in value, he sailed back around the cape of Africa. When he finally dropped anchor in Plymouth Harbour, he had completed a voyage around the world. The shareholders who had risked their money on that venture were now rich beyond their wildest dreams; they made a profit on their money of some 4700 per cent!

The Queen's encouragement

The Queen herself greatly encouraged this expansion of trade and she even lent some of the Treasury's money to the Levant Company to finance voyages to Turkey and other Middle-eastern countries. When trade with the Levant declined, the same merchants set up the East India Company in 1600. Although the first voyages were a failure, by about 1614 the company was making profits of over 300 per cent. In the following centuries, England's empire in India was founded through the exploits of the East India Company.

The Indian town of Pomeiooc in Virginia, North America, by John White, one of the early settlers in the colony. Many of the English colonists who went to seek their fortune in Virginia were fascinated by the American Indians and their way of life. Some, like White, depicted and described their houses, clothes and costumes.

Voyages for colonization

Voyages for trade were frequently profitable, but Sir Walter Raleigh's dream of setting up a colony in North America was not. Personally, he and his half-brother, Sir Humphrey Gilbert, lost their fortunes on the English colony of Virginia. The colony was eventually taken over by a company, but it did not make any profits for its shareholders for some time. Unexpectedly, tobacco became fashionable and the investors became rich with a crop which has remained popular and profitable to this day.

A play on a topical subject

Shakespeare found the story for *The Merchant of Venice* in a collection of Italian stories by Ser Giovanni called *Il Pecorone*. Whether he read it in the Italian or in a translation which is now lost we do not know. There are a number of reasons why he might have chosen this tale about a Jewish moneylender, a prosperous merchant and a poor nobleman who wins the hand of a rich lady.

Why Shakespeare wrote this play

Sometime before Shakespeare wrote the play in 1596 or 1597, his friend, the playwright Christopher Marlowe, had written a play called *The Jew of Malta*. This became very popular with the Elizabethans and was performed time and time again. Around this time, too, there was a real-life trial of a Jewish man from Portugal, Roderigo Lopez. He was Queen Elizabeth's doctor and was accused of treason for attempting to kill her. Although he was probably innocent, he was found guilty in 1594 and executed. The trial was much talked about at the time, and Shakespeare's audience would have responded to this story about a heartless Jew. It reflected their feeling of patriotism for the Queen at that time.

Jews in England

In Shakespeare's day, very few Jewish people lived in England. This was because, since the reign of Edward I, they were banned from the country unless they were willing to become Christians. Those who remained in England were generally ordinary, peaceable citizens who probably quietly practised their own religion without offending anyone – even

In the 16th century, gold and silver coins were weighed and their value recorded, according to the amount of precious metal they contained. Nowadays, the silver and gold content of coins is small and throughout most of the world paper notes are used for all but the smallest denominations.

This woodcut depicts Roderigo Lopez, Queen Elizabeth's Jewish doctor, who was falsely accused of treason.

though they had been baptised Christians.

In European cities, such as Venice, there was quite a large Jewish population. In the Middle Ages, many did become moneylenders or pawnbrokers. In countries or cities which relied on trade, the authorities encouraged this, because the Christian law which forbade moneylending for profit did not apply to Jewish people. Although some became rich like Shylock, most did not because the governments demanded heavy taxes from them.

10

This view of Venice and the Rialto Bridge was made by Giovanni Antonio Canaletto in the 18th century. The bridge led to the Rialto, the building similar to the Royal Exchange in London, where Venetian gentlemen and merchants met twice a day. Shylock mentions the Rialto in The Merchant of Venice.

Disapproval of moneylenders

The whole business of moneylending was of particular interest to the Elizabethans. Up until 1571, it had been against the law to lend money and charge interest on it. Businessmen and many noblemen needed money, however, and they were forced to borrow it and pay high rates of interest. Just as people today complain about high taxes or bank charges, so in those days borrowing money with interest was the topic of the day.

Books and pamphlets were written about it and although usury (the lending of money with interest) was regarded as a sin, it became legal because it was necessary for trade. The rate of interest permitted by law was 10 per cent but, of course, many people paid far more than that – just as they do today.

Some distinguished borrowers

The celebrated Elizabethan courtier, Sir Philip Sidney, owed the present-day equivalent of about £120,000 in debts, and the Earl of Essex, the Queen's favourite, owed more than double that amount. Queen Elizabeth herself had to borrow very large sums from European bankers and sometimes paid up to 14 per cent interest. Shakespeare's acting company built the Globe Theatre on borrowed money, and repaying the interest was a heavy burden for the theatre. So for Shakespeare, as a shareholder in the Globe, and for the tradesmen and noblemen who sat in the galleries, usury was an important issue; they would have appreciated the problems of Antonio and Bassanio in *The Merchant of Venice*.

It was not unusual in those days for young noblemen like Bassanio to borrow money to court a lady with a fortune. If, like Bassanio, they were successful, their money problems were solved.

Robert Devereux, 2nd Earl of Essex, was for a time the Queen's favourite. With an expensive lifestyle to maintain at court, Essex spent far beyond his means. He was forced to borrow heavily from moneylenders.

Shylock the man

Shylock is one of Shakespeare's most famous characters and he is meant to be a villain and a sinner. As always, however, even the most evil characters in Shakespeare's plays, like Macbeth, show signs of human feeling from time to time. In Shylock, we can see how lonely and painful it must have been to be insulted, simply because of your religion – when even kind men like Antonio thought it normal to abuse Jewish people. Shylock was an outcast in society, part of a under-privileged minority who were not even allowed to own land. Although he is a villainous man, we cannot help feeling a little sorry for him when even his own daughter leaves him to become a Christian.

The story of The Merchant of Venice

Antonio, a merchant of Venice, is filled with a strange sadness. His friends think that he is worried about the ships he has abroad, in which he has put all his money. Antonio dismisses this idea and says he is simply sad by nature.

Antonio's sadness

I hold the world but as the world, Gratiano;
A stage where every man must play a part,
And mine a sad one.

Act 1 Sc i

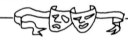

Bassanio's problems
Bassanio is a handsome young nobleman who has fallen into debt. He explains that without money he cannot woo the beautiful heiress Portia whom he admires. Antonio, who loves his friend dearly, cannot lend Bassanio the money personally, but offers to borrow money for his friend from Shylock, the Jewish moneylender.

Portia and her suitors
Portia is rich and beautiful and lives on her estate at Belmont, a short distance away from Venice by sea. She is bored and discontented because she is not allowed to choose the husband she wants. In her father's will, he sets up a test for her suitors. They must choose between three caskets, one of silver, one of gold and one of lead. Only when they open the casket they have chosen will they – and Portia – know if they have won her hand in marriage. So far, she has not been very impressed with her suitors and speaks scathingly about them.

14

Portia describes one suitor

Nerissa *How like you the young German, the Duke of Saxony's nephew?*
Portia *Very vilely in the morning when he is sober, and most vilely in the afternoon, when he is drunk: when he is best, he is a little worse than a man, and when he is worst, he is little better than a beast.*

Act I Sc ii

Shylock strikes a bargain

Shylock hates Antonio because he sometimes lends out money for nothing, while Shylock earns his living by lending money and charging interest. He is surprised when Antonio asks for a loan because Antonio has always spurned and abused him. Hatching a plot, Shylock agrees to lend 3000

15

ducats on one condition: if the debt is not paid, Shylock will demand one pound of Antonio's flesh 'cut off and taken in what part of your body pleaseth me.'

An exotic suitor for Portia

The most magnificent of Portia's suitors is the Prince of Morocco, who arrives at Belmont with courtiers all dressed in white. He hopes that Portia will not reject him because of his dark skin – but she, of course, has no choice in the matter. She leads him to the three caskets. Before he chooses, he must swear that, whatever the outcome, he will never court another woman.

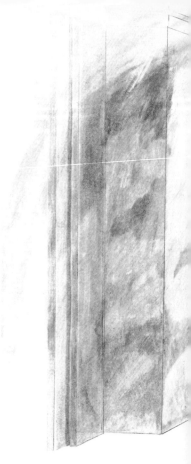

Morocco's appeal to Portia

Mislike me not for my complexion,
The shadow'd livery of the burnish'd sun,
To whom I am a neighbour and near bred.
Bring me the fairest creature northward born,
Where Phoebus' fire scarce thaws the icicles,
And let us make incision for your love,
To prove whose blood is reddest, his or mine.

Act II Sc i

A clown leaves his master

Back in Venice, Launcelot Gobbo, Shylock's clown, has decided to leave his master because of his miserliness. The poor but generous-hearted Bassanio agrees to take Launcelot into his service.

Gratiano, another young nobleman, pleads with Bassanio to be allowed to go to Belmont with him. Bassanio is reluctant because Gratiano is high-spirited and a chatterbox; he fears that Gratiano's talkative manner might upset people at Belmont, and ruin his chances with Portia. In the end, Bassanio is too soft-hearted to refuse his friend's request.

16

Introducing Shylock's daughter, Jessica

Shylock's daughter, Jessica, bids farewell to Launcelot and gives him a message for her lover, Lorenzo. She asks him to rescue her from her father's house that night and promises to bring money and jewels.

Shylock is uneasy and reluctant to leave his house. He fears something is going to happen – 'For I did dream of moneybags tonight', he says. He knows that a masque (a theatrical entertainment) is to take place in Venice that night and he warns Jessica to keep the house locked up.

Exit Jessica with the jewels

As promised, Lorenzo and his friends wait outside Shylock's house. They are dressed for the masque so that their faces are hidden. When Jessica appears at the window, she throws down a casket containing jewels and money. She herself follows, dressed in boy's clothes; it has been arranged that she will pretend to be Lorenzo's torch-bearer. Lorenzo declares his love for this brave girl.

> **Lorenzo declares his love for Jessica**
> *Beshrew me, but I love her heartily;*
> *For she is wise, if I can judge of her,*
> *And fair she is, if that mine eyes be true,*
> *And true she is, as she hath prov'd herself;*
> *And therefore, like herself, wise, fair, and true,*
> *Shall she be placed in my constant soul.*　　Act II Sc vi

Morocco chooses the casket

Back in Belmont, the Prince of Morocco is about to choose the casket. Each one has an inscription which he reads. If he chooses the right one, it will contain a portrait of Portia.

> **The inscriptions on the caskets**　　Act II Sc vii
> *This first, of gold, which this inscription bears:*
> Who chooseth me shall gain what many men desire.
> *The second, silver, which this promise carries:*
> Who chooseth me shall get as much as he deserves.
> *This third, dull lead, with warning all as blunt:*
> Who chooseth me must give and hazard all he hath.

The prince chooses the gold casket because he believes that all the world must desire Portia. Alas, when he opens it, it contains a skull with a message.

> **The golden casket's message**
> *All that glisters is not gold;*　*Had you been as wise as bold,*
> *Often have you heard that told:*　*Young in limbs, in judgment old,*
> *Many a man his life hath sold*　*Your answer had not been inscroll'd, –*
> *But my outside to behold:*　*Fare you well; your suit is cold.*
> *Gilded tombs do worm infold.*
> 　　　　　　　　　　　　　　Act II Sc vii

The Prince has failed and he leaves, grieved and disappointed.

Shylock's reason for revenge

He hath disgraced me, and hindered me half a million, laughed at my losses, mocked at my gains, scorned my nation, thwarted my bargains, cooled my friends, heated mine enemies; and what's his reason? I am a Jew. Hath not a Jew eyes? hath not a Jew hands, organs, dimensions, senses, affections, passions? fed with the same food, hurt with the same weapons, subject to the same diseases, healed by the same means, warmed and cooled by the same winter and summer, as a Christian is? If you prick us, do we not bleed? if you tickle us, do we not laugh? if you poison us, do we not die? and if you wrong us, shall we not revenge? If we are like you in the rest, we will resemble you in that.

Act III Sci

Bassanio makes his way to Belmont

Bassanio with Gratiano sets sails for Belmont while another suitor, the Prince of Arragon, takes his chances with the casket. A conceited man, he chooses the silver casket, but finds only a fool's head when he opens it.

Disastrous news in Venice

In Venice, news has spread that Antonio has lost one of his most valuable ships. Shylock vows he will now extract his pound of flesh. He is driven by revenge because Antonio has always hated him for being a Jew.

Shylock is more concerned by the loss of his money than by the loss of his daughter. He hears, too, that she has wasted his money, even selling a ring which had sentimental value for him.

Bassanio chooses a casket

Portia is reluctant for Bassanio to choose the casket. She has fallen in love with him and fears that he will fail the test – but Bassanio is impatient to know his fate. As he goes to the caskets, Portia instructs her musicians to play sweet music.

The musicians' song

Tell me where is fancy bred,
Or in the heart, or in the head?
How begot, how nourished?

   Reply, reply.

It is engender'd in the eyes,
With gazing fed; and fancy dies
In the cradle where it lies.
   Let us all ring fancy's knell.
   I'll begin it – Ding, dong, bell.

Act III Sc ii

Bassanio chooses the lead casket, opens it and finds Portia's portrait. Portia humbly offers herself and all her worldly goods to him and gives him a ring as a love token. Bassanio can hardly believe his fortune.

Portia's acceptance

You see me, Lord Bassanio, where I stand,
Such as I am . . . but the full sum of me
Is sum of nothing; which, to term in gross,
Is an unlesson'd girl, unschool'd, unpractis'd;
Happy in this, she is not yet so old
But she may learn; happier than this,
She is not bred so dull but she can learn;
Happiest of all is that her gentle spirit
Commits itself to yours to be directed,
As from her lord, her governor, her king.
Myself and what is mine to you and yours
Is now converted . . . .

Act III Sc ii

To the couple's surprise and delight, Nerissa, Portia's lady-in-waiting, announces that she and Gratiano have fallen in love.

News of Antonio

Their happiness is interrupted when news arrives of Antonio's troubles; he is to appear in court before the Duke of Venice. Bassanio departs immediately to be with his friend, while Nerissa and Portia make plans to go to a nearby monastery to await the return of the men. In fact, Portia has quite different ideas. She intends to go to Venice dressed as a young lawyer to defend Antonio. She leaves the care of her house in Belmont to Lorenzo and Jessica.

In the Venetian courtroom

Antonio knows that the Duke of Venice cannot help him because the bond is a legal one, and the law must be upheld. He prepares to meet his fate.

In the courtroom, the Duke tries to reason with Shylock. Bassanio offers double the bond money but Shylock will not be moved.

Antonio on his fate

I am a tainted wether of the flock,
Meetest for death: the weakest kind of fruit
Drops earliest to the ground; and so let me:
You cannot better be employ'd, Bassanio,
Than to live still, and write mine epitaph.

Act IV Sc i

Enter the young "doctor of law"

Just then, Portia, dressed as a young lawyer, arrives with her "clerk", Nerissa. She informs the court that she has been sent by Dr. Bellario from Padua to fight the case. She admits that Shylock has the law on his side, but asks him to be merciful.

Portia's plea for mercy

The quality of mercy is not strain'd,
It droppeth as the gentle rain from heaven
Upon the place beneath: it is twice bless'd;
It blesseth him that gives, and him that takes:
'Tis mightiest in the mightiest; it becomes
The throned monarch better than his crown;
His sceptre shows the force of temporal power,
The attribute to awe and majesty,
Wherein doth sit the dread and fear of kings;
But mercy is above this sceptred sway,
It is enthroned in the hearts of kings,
It is an attribute to God himself,
And earthly power doth then show likest God's
When mercy seasons justice.

Act IV Sci

How Shylock is defeated

Portia then utters a warning. In taking the pound of flesh, Shylock must not shed "one drop of Christian blood" – otherwise, all his property will be confiscated. Shylock realizes he cannot win; he is defeated. Although the Duke allows him to live, Shylock leaves the court a broken man.

A gift for the lawyer

The young lawyer refuses a gift of money, but presses Bassanio for the ring given to him by Portia. Reluctantly, he parts with it, as does Gratiano with his, which goes to the lawyer's clerk.

25

Lorenzo on the power of music

How sweet the moonlight sleeps upon this bank!
Here will we sit, and let the sounds of music
Creep in our ears; soft stillness and the night
Become the touches of sweet harmony.
Sit Jessica: look, how the floor of heaven
Is thick inlaid with patines of bright gold:
There's not the smallest orb which thou behold'st
But in his motion like an angel sings,
Still quiring to the young-eyed cherubins;
Such harmony is in immortal souls;
But, whilst this muddy vesture of decay
Doth grossly close it in, we cannot hear it . . .
The man that hath no music in himself,
Nor is not mov'd with concord of sweet sounds,
Is fit for treasons, stratagems, and spoils . . .
Let no such man be trusted.

Act v Sc i

Harmony – and disharmony – in Belmont

As Lorenzo and Jessica linger at night in the garden at Belmont, he describes the power of music. Soon after, Nerissa and Portia arrive home, followed by Bassanio, Gratiano and Antonio. Portia makes Antonio most welcome, but then a quarrel breaks out between the young couples over the loss of the wedding rings. Portia pretends to be very angry – but then reveals that she has the ring, explaining, to the men's amazement, that she and Nerissa were the lawyer and his clerk. News arrives that Antonio's ships have arrived safely at port, and the joy of everyone is complete.

The play's characters

Portia

Shylock

Portia

Portia is very beautiful and extremely rich, and suitors come from 'the four corners of the earth' to woo her. At the beginning of the play, she is rather bored and dissatisfied, but after she is won by Bassanio her real personality emerges. Intelligent and quick-witted, she decides to help Antonio, and as a result of her cleverness in the courtroom she saves the day. She is a very capable lady, and generous with both her love and her money. Bassanio is especially fortunate to have won such a prize.

Shylock

Thou call'dst me dog before thou hadst a cause, But, since I am a dog, beware my fangs.

Shylock is the best-known character in this play. He is a forceful but villainous person who is driven by hate and greed. Although he has many reasons to hate Antonio, who spurns him because he is Jewish, his desire for revenge is fuelled by great bitterness and anger. He is a man who has no warmth or love in him, not even for his own daughter. He displays little human feeling of any kind except when he talks with passion about his treatment as a Jew.

In Portia's praise
In Belmont is a lady richly left,
And she is fair, and, fairer than that word,
Of wondrous virtues: sometimes from her eyes
I did receive fair speechless messages:
Her name is Portia.

Act I Sc i

Antonio

In sooth, I know not why I am so sad: It wearies me; you say it wearies you;

Although the play is named after him, Antonio plays a fairly small part in the play. He seems a rather sad figure because, although he has close friends like Bassanio, he has no wife or lover. His kindness and generosity to his young friend is boundless. He is, without doubt, the most noble and unselfish person in the entire play, and in the end gets his just reward.

Bassanio

Although Bassanio is a handsome young man who is chivalrous, sociable and generous-spirited, many people have criticised him for being a fortune hunter and a spendthrift. He seems to have no money of his own, although he has an extravagant lifestyle. He relies, first, on the generosity of Antonio, who borrows money for him; after he has won Portia, it is her money which will pay his debts. This would not have worried the Elizabethans who knew of many young noblemen who lived beyond their means. Bassanio is a true gentleman and a loving friend to Antonio; and his warmth and honesty make him a worthy hero.

Bassanio

Antonio

Why Shylock hates Antonio
Signior Antonio, many a time and oft
In the Rialto you have rated me
About my moneys and my usances...
You call me misbeliever, cut-throat dog,
And spet upon my Jewish gaberdine,
And all for use of that which is mine own.

Act I Sc iii

29

Lorenzo

Jessica

Lorenzo

Lorenzo is a handsome, dashing young man. Having fallen in love with Jessica, he rescues her and elopes with her. His easy and friendly ways are valued by Portia, who leaves the couple in charge of her house at Belmont. Lorenzo's conversations with Jessica are full of lovely poetry and playfulness; they are a couple whom we feel sure will live happily ever after.

Jessica

There is more difference between thy (Shylock's) *flesh and hers than between jet and ivory.*

Jessica shares none of her father's characteristics. She is young and pretty with a sense of fun, and she is rather impulsive. Although we cannot blame her for eloping with Lorenzo, we feel uneasy about her stealing her father's money and jewels – especially when she spends the money so extravagantly. Her sunny, open nature, however, is very winning, and since Shakespeare sympathises with her we do, too.

Lorenzo talks of love

The moon shines bright: in such a night as this,
When the sweet wind did gently kiss the trees
And they did make no noise, in such a night
Troilus methinks mounted the Troyan walls,
And sigh'd his soul toward the Grecian tents,
Where Cressid lay that night.

Act v Sc i

The life and plays of Shakespeare

Life of Shakespeare

1564 William Shakespeare born at Stratford-upon-Avon.

1582 Shakespeare marries Anne Hathaway, eight years his senior.

1583 Shakespeare's daughter, Susanna, is born.

1585 The twins, Hamnet and Judith, are born.

1587 Shakespeare goes to London.

1591-2 Shakespeare writes *The Comedy of Errors*. He is becoming well-known as an actor and writer.

1592 Theatres closed because of plague.

1593-4 Shakespeare writes *Titus Andronicus* and *The Taming of the Shrew*: he is member of the theatrical company, the Chamberlain's Men.

1594-5 Shakespeare writes *Romeo and Juliet*.

1595 Shakespeare writes *A Midsummer Night's Dream*.

1595-6 Shakespeare writes *Richard II*.

1596 Shakespeare's son, Hamnet, dies. He writes *King John* and *The Merchant of Venice*.

1597 Shakespeare buys New Place in Stratford.

1597-8 Shakespeare writes *Henry IV*.

1599 Shakespeare's theatre company opens the Globe Theatre.

1599-1600 Shakespeare writes *As You Like It*, *Henry V* and *Twelfth Night*.

1600-01 Shakespeare writes *Hamlet*.

1602-03 Shakespeare writes *All's Well That Ends Well*.

1603 Elizabeth I dies. James I becomes king. Theatres closed because of plague.

1603-04 Shakespeare writes *Othello*.

1605 Theatres closed because of plague.

1605-06 Shakespeare writes *Macbeth* and *King Lear*.

1606-07 Shakespeare writes *Antony and Cleopatra*.

1607 Susanna Shakespeare marries Dr John Hall. Theatres closed because of plague.

1608 Shakespeare's granddaughter, Elizabeth Hall, is born.

1609 *Sonnets* published. Theatres closed because of plague.

1610 Theatres closed because of plague. Shakespeare gives up his London lodgings and retires to Stratford.

1611-12 Shakespeare writes *The Tempest*.

1613 Globe Theatre burns to the ground during a performance of Henry VIII.

1616 Shakespeare dies on 23 April.

Shakespeare's plays

The Comedy of Errors
Love's Labour's Lost
Henry VI Part 2
Henry VI Part 3
Henry VI Part 1
Richard III
Titus Andronicus
The Taming of the Shrew
The Two Gentlemen of Verona
Romeo and Juliet
Richard II
A Midsummer Night's Dream
King John
The Merchant of Venice
Henry IV Part 1
Henry IV Part 2
Much Ado About Nothing
Henry V
Julius Caesar
As You Like It
Twelfth Night
Hamlet
The Merry Wives of Windsor
Troilus and Cressida
All's Well That Ends Well
Othello
Measure for Measure
King Lear
Macbeth
Antony and Cleopatra
Timon of Athens
Coriolanus
Pericles
Cymbeline
The Winter's Tale
The Tempest
Henry VIII

Index

Acknowledgments

The publishers would like to thank Morag Gibson and Patrick Rudd for their help in producing this book.

Picture credits

p.1 Governors of Royal Shakespeare Theatre, p3 National Portrait Gallery, p.5 Private collection (photo Bridgeman Art Library), p.7 British Museum (photo Bridgeman Art Library), p.9 Musée des Beaux-Arts, Valenciennes (photo Bridgeman Art Library), p.12 National Portrait Gallery.